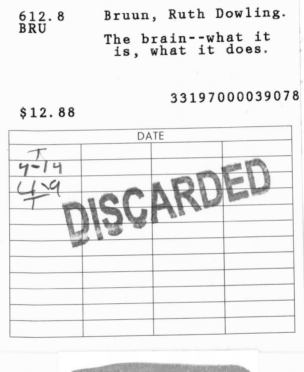

Greenwillow
Read-alone

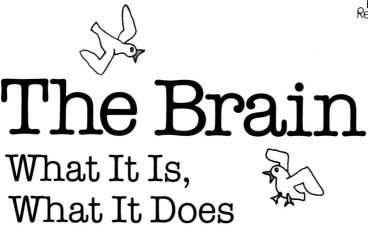

The Brain

What It Is,
What It Does

Dr. Ruth Dowling Bruun
and Dr. Bertel Bruun

illustrated by Peter Bruun

Greenwillow Books, New York

To our first grandchild/child

—R. D. B., B. B., and P. B.

The artwork was preseparated and printed in two colors.
The text type is Plantin.

Text copyright © 1989 by Ruth Dowling Bruun and Bertel Bruun
Illustrations copyright © 1989 by Peter Bruun   All rights reserved.
No part of this book may be reproduced or utilized in any
form or by any means, electronic or mechanical, including
photocopying, recording or by any information storage
and retrieval system, without permission in writing from the
Publisher, Greenwillow Books, a division of William Morrow
& Company, Inc., 105 Madison Avenue, New York, N.Y. 10016.
Printed in the United States of America
First Edition   10 9 8 7 6 5 4 3 2

Library of Congress Cataloging-in-Publication Data

Bruun, Ruth Dowling.
The brain—what it is, what it does /
by Ruth Dowling Bruun and Bertel Bruun;
pictures by Peter Bruun
(A Greenwillow read-alone book)
p.   cm
Summary: Introduces the human brain, its parts,
how it works, and what it helps us accomplish,
and discusses several animal brains.
ISBN 0-688-08453-2.   ISBN 0-688-08454-0 (lib. bdg.)
1. Brain—Juvenile literature.   [1. Brain.]
I. Bruun, Bertel.   II. Title.
III. Series: Greenwillow read-alone books.
QP376.B78 1989   612′.82—dc19   88-21182   CIP   AC

Contents

1: Introduction

Have you ever thought about what makes you able to think? Or able to talk, walk, or ride a bicycle? Or what makes you breathe? Or what makes you see, hear, smell, or feel? Or what makes you dream? Or what makes you feel happy or sad or angry?

Your brain does all these things
and many, many more.
It is the most important part
of your body.
It not only makes your body work,
but your brain is what makes you
who you are.

You might be able
to get a new heart,
but even if doctors
could give you a new brain,
you wouldn't want it
because then you
wouldn't be you anymore.

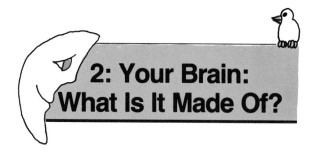

2: Your Brain: What Is It Made Of?

Your brain is made up of billions and billions of tiny nerve cells. They are so small that you can see them only through a microscope. There are so many that if they were placed end to end  they would reach to the moon and back again.

A nerve cell is called a neuron.

It looks like this. - - - - - - →

It has a body, a long tail,

and many branches.

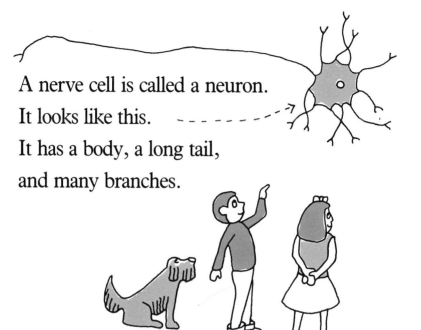

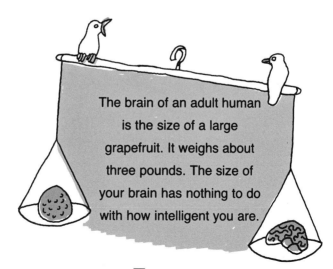

The brain of an adult human is the size of a large grapefruit. It weighs about three pounds. The size of your brain has nothing to do with how intelligent you are.

Each nerve cell is connected with
thousands of other nerve cells
by these branches,
which almost touch each other.

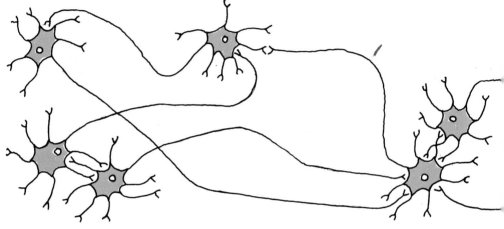

From the end of each branch
chemicals are sent out and
picked up by the nearest branch
of another neuron.

When a chemical message
is received by a neuron,
it is carried through
its branches
by electricity.

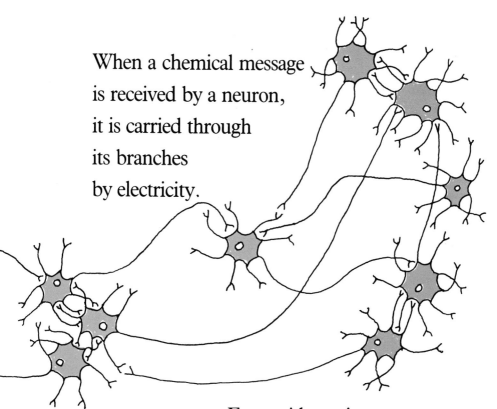

Even with a microscope
you cannot see
neurons sending messages.
But millions of messages
are being sent
and received every second.
This is how the brain
does its work.

The brain doesn't only
send messages
from one neuron
to another.
It also sends and
receives messages
to and from
the rest of your body
to make your body work.

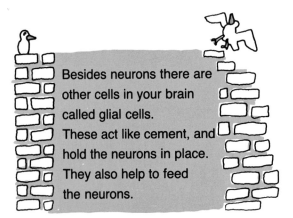

Besides neurons there are
other cells in your brain
called glial cells.
These act like cement, and
hold the neurons in place.
They also help to feed
the neurons.

How the Parts of the Brain Work

The brain has three parts:
the cerebrum, the cerebellum,
and the brain stem.

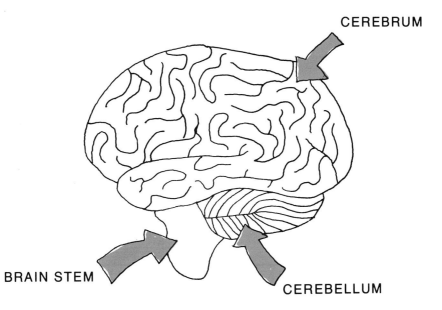

CEREBRUM

BRAIN STEM

CEREBELLUM

Each part does something different.

CEREBRUM

The cerebrum is
the biggest part
of your brain.
Different areas
of the cerebrum
enable you to do
different things.

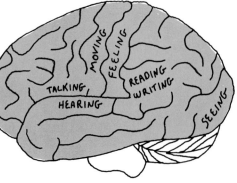

One part is for seeing,
and another is for hearing.

Your cerebrum is where
all your thoughts are formed.

Deep in your brain is a part
for smelling and tasting.
Other parts receive messages
from your skin about heat and cold,
sharpness and dullness, and
shapes and textures.
Still other parts make you able
to understand what you are seeing,
hearing, smelling, tasting, and touching.
Certain parts of your cerebrum
make the muscles of your body move.

CEREBELLUM

The cerebellum is another part
of your brain.
It is under the back part
of your cerebrum.

The cerebellum controls
your coordination.

It helps you move your arms
and legs smoothly.
The cerebellum also helps you
keep your balance

so you don't fall down.

The brain stem has nerves that
control the way your heart beats,
your breathing, and the many
other things that your body does
without your being aware of them.

You don't have to think
about making your heart beat
or your stomach work.
In fact, you can't control these things
even if you do think about them.
Your brain stem does all that.
It takes care of your body
while your cerebrum does the thinking.

The brain stem also connects
the cerebrum and
the cerebellum
with the spinal cord,
which runs down your back.
In the spinal cord
there are neuron branches
running to and from
the brain.
There are also
other neurons with branches
to all the parts of your body.

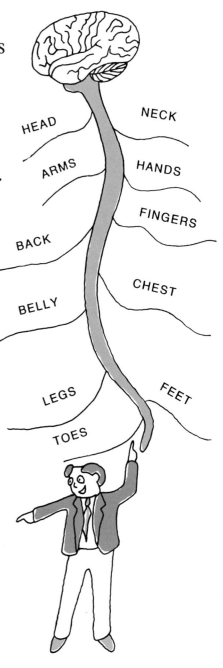

HEAD

NECK

ARMS

HANDS

FINGERS

BACK

CHEST

BELLY

LEGS

FEET

TOES

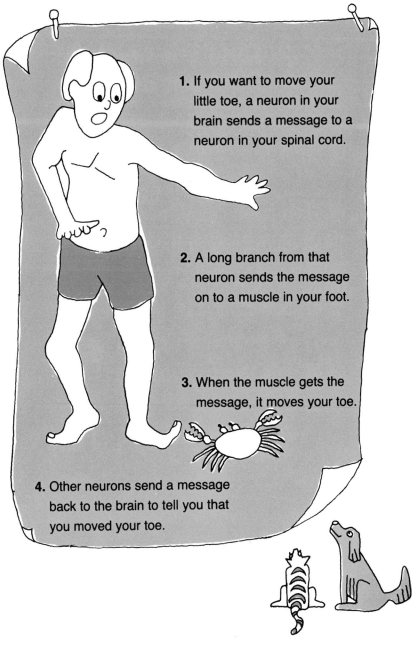

1. If you want to move your little toe, a neuron in your brain sends a message to a neuron in your spinal cord.

2. A long branch from that neuron sends the message on to a muscle in your foot.

3. When the muscle gets the message, it moves your toe.

4. Other neurons send a message back to the brain to tell you that you moved your toe.

3: Different Animals, Different Brains

You might think that
all animals have brains.
But nearly half of all types
of animals have no brain at all.
These animals don't even have heads.
Most of them, germs for example,
are so small that you cannot see them
without a microscope.

Jellyfish

There are also bigger animals
that have no brains.
Jellyfish have nerves
all over their bodies,
but they have
no brains.

But even without a brain
a jellyfish can do many things.
It can search for food.
It can sense danger
and move away from it.

It can even sting you
if it senses that you are an enemy.

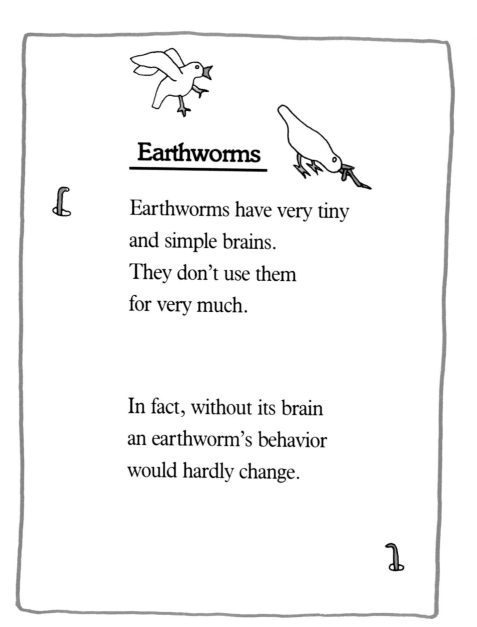

Earthworms

Earthworms have very tiny
and simple brains.
They don't use them
for very much.

In fact, without its brain
an earthworm's behavior
would hardly change.

Dinosaurs

Some scientists believe that certain
big dinosaurs had two brains,
one in the head and one in the tail.
This may have been because
the tail was so far from the head
that it would have taken too long
to send messages back and forth.
If one of these dinosaurs
needed to move its tail quickly,
the tail brain could take charge.

Fish

Fish have brains, but a fish brain
has only a very small cerebrum.
That is why fish cannot think
the way humans can.

Birds

Birds have more
advanced brains
than fish.
A large part of a bird's cerebrum
is used for sight.

 Birds have much better sight
than people do.

Mammals

Dogs and cats have brains
that are more like human brains.
In fact any mammal has a bigger cerebrum
than a fish, reptile, or bird of the same size.

Dogs' brains have much bigger areas
for smell than human brains.
Smell is much more important
in a dog's life than in yours.

Though dogs can remember and learn,
they cannot create new ideas.

4: How You Think and Learn

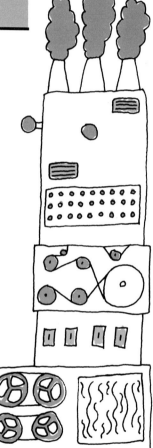

The human brain is like
a very complicated machine
or computer.
No one knows exactly
how the brain is able to think.
When you think, your brain
is using information
that it has learned
and stored
for future use.

For example, imagine that
you meet a dog named Fluffy.

Your eyes tell the seeing part
of your brain what Fluffy looks like.

Your nose tells the smelling part
of your brain what Fluffy smells like.

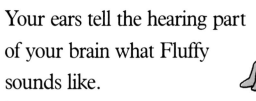

Your ears tell the hearing part
of your brain what Fluffy
sounds like.

Your skin tells the feeling part
of your brain what Fluffy feels like.

All this information
is put together in your brain
to form a memory of Fluffy.

Just the name Fluffy makes you
remember in an instant
what it was like to see, hear,
smell, and feel Fluffy.

— FLUFFY!

When you think,
your brain cells are sending
messages to each other.

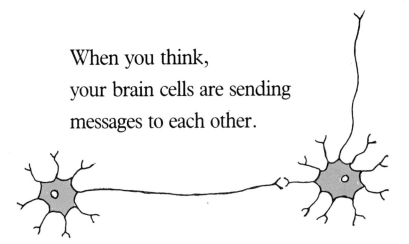

Some scientists believe that
messages follow certain patterns
for certain thoughts.
If this is so, then thinking
is like going through a maze
inside your own brain.

Sometimes you follow
the same pathways
over and over again.
The more you do this,
the easier it gets to follow them.

You learned the alphabet this way.
First the letters
just looked like lines.
They didn't mean anything to you.

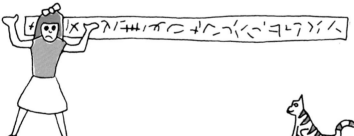

Then someone showed you
that three lines put together
like this - - - - - - -> made a letter.

You may have had to be shown
over and over.

Suddenly one day you looked
at the letter A and
you knew what it was.

You learn how to ride a bike
the same way.

You try it over

and over

until your brain
moves all of your muscles
in the right way.

When you are good at something

like riding a bicycle

 or swimming

or tying your shoelaces,

part of your brain
can be thinking
of how to do it
while another part
can be thinking about other things.

Another way of learning
is by figuring things out.
Instead of your brain cells
following the same old patterns,
they try out new ones.
Just like going through a maze,
the new pathways
sometimes lead to dead ends.

But other times you find
a new way through the maze
and you have a new idea
that works!
This new idea can be no more
than a shortcut to your home,
or it can be as important as
the invention of the wheel.

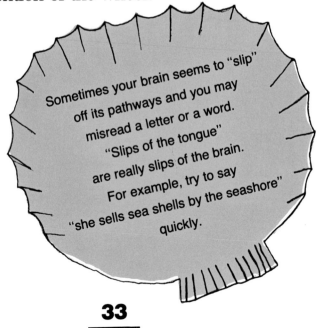

Sometimes your brain seems to "slip" off its pathways and you may misread a letter or a word. "Slips of the tongue" are really slips of the brain. For example, try to say "she sells sea shells by the seashore" quickly.

5: Intelligence

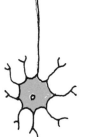

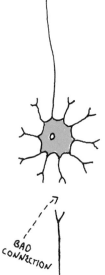

Some people's brains
are quicker at learning
than others.
We don't know why this is.
It could be because
some people's neurons
connect better with each other.

GOOD CONNECTION

BAD CONNECTION

We do know that
you can learn things faster
when you concentrate on them.

When your brain is distracted
by other thoughts
it cannot store information as well.

This is one reason that
you remember some things
and forget others.

When you were born
you had all the neurons
you will ever have.
Human beings
don't grow new neurons.
Some other animals do,
however.

A bird grows new nerve cells
when it learns to sing every spring.

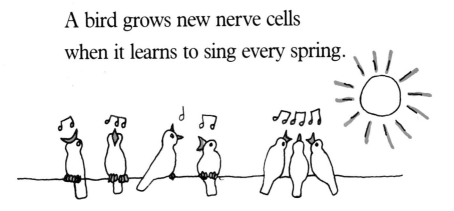

But every winter,
when it stops singing,
the part of the bird's brain
that controls singing shrinks.

Even though humans
cannot grow new brain cells,
they have a big advantage
over other animals.
Animals can save information
only in their brains,
but humans have learned
to store information
outside their brains.
This is what books, videotapes,
records, and computers are for.

A mother lion has to teach her cubs
how to hunt by being with them
all the time.

But you can learn things
when your mother isn't there,
or things she doesn't even know.

BUILD—
IT—
YOUR—
SELF—
BIRD—
HOUSE.

6: Feelings

Some days you feel happy.

Some days you feel sad.

Most of the time you know why
you are happy or sad,
or why you are angry
or anxious, frightened or surprised.
When something happens to cause
one of these feelings,
your brain makes your body respond
in a certain way.

When you are frightened
your brain will tell your heart
to pump faster
and will give your muscles
extra energy
so that you are ready
to fight

or to run away.

When you are sad
your brain will tell your eyes
to make tears.

And when you are happy
your brain will tell
your mouth muscles to smile
or your throat muscles to laugh.

Sometimes you may feel
sad or happy
for no special reason.
Such feelings usually go away
in a little while.
But you may have known people
who had to take medicine
to stop their brain
from making them sad.
Sometimes the brain
needs medicine
to keep its chemistry
properly balanced.

7: Sleep

During your lifetime
you spend more than one third
of your time asleep.
When you sleep, your body is resting
but your brain may not be.
Nobody knows for certain.
In fact, sleep is not something
your body does,
it is something your brain does.

All night your brain is going
through different kinds of sleep
over and over again.

We know about this by
recordings of "brain waves."
These brain waves are made
by the electricity in the neurons
in your brain.

When you are awake and relaxed
your brain waves look like this.

Sleep begins with drowsiness.
Then your brain waves look like this.

You feel your muscles relaxing,
and your thoughts drift off
as you enter a light sleep.
Then your brain waves look like this.

Gradually you go into
a deeper and deeper sleep.
Your brain waves look like this.

Because the waves
are now coming very slowly,
your brain seems to be resting.
But then something different happens.
Your brain starts
a different kind of sleep,
the type that produces dreams.
The brain waves look like this.

Dreams

Dreaming periods may be
as short as ten minutes.
On rare occasions they
may last for almost an hour.
You usually have
four or five of them
every night.
In between,
your brain
seems to be resting.

During dreaming sleep
parts of your body are not resting.
Your heart beats faster
and you breathe faster, too.
Your eyes move around rapidly,
almost as if you were awake,
but your eyelids are closed
and the main muscles of your body
are completely relaxed.

Have you ever tried
to run away in a dream
and not been able to move a muscle?
This is because in dreaming sleep
your leg muscles
are completely relaxed.

Relaxed muscles
in your mouth and throat
are what make you snore.
When you breathe in and out,
the air makes these muscles quiver
and this makes a noise

No one really knows
the reason for dreams.
A long time ago people thought
that dreams foretold the future.
Now we think that they are probably
a way for your brain
to think some more about things
that have happened
when you were awake.

Many things that happen to you
during the day will be in your dreams,
but they will be all mixed up.

Whatever the reason
for dreams may be,
we know that normal people
dream every night.
If you think you didn't dream
one night, it is only because
it is easy to forget your dreams.

Animal Dreams

Many animals dream.
Birds and mammals have dreaming
and non-dreaming periods of sleep
just as people do.
But we don't know
what they dream about.

Does a cat dream
of chasing mice,

or a dog dream
of chasing cats?

Probably.
Other animals, like fish,
don't even sleep,
although they do rest.

How Much Sleep
Do You Need?

When you are very young
you need more sleep
than when you are older.
Newborn babies sleep
almost all the time.
They wake only when
they are hungry or wet.

By the time you are ready for school
you need to sleep only at night,
but you still need more sleep
than an adult.

If you don't get enough sleep
your brain will not work
as well as it can.

8: Food for Thought

Your brain is different
from other parts
of your body.
As you grow, your body
makes many new cells
of different kinds.
Your brain does not.
The only reason
your brain grows in size
is that the cells themselves grow.

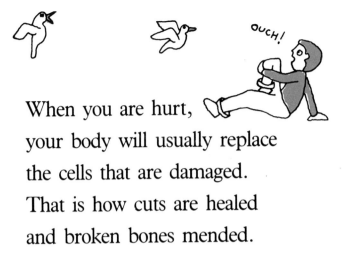

When you are hurt,
your body will usually replace
the cells that are damaged.
That is how cuts are healed
and broken bones mended.

But your brain cannot replace
nerve cells that are damaged.
This is why
you must take very good care
of your brain.

Your brain needs a lot of energy
to do all the work it does.
To keep it healthy you must eat well.
When you are hungry
you will feel cranky and tired.
You won't be able to think clearly
until you eat.

Not only does your brain
need good food in order
to work well,
it also needs to be protected
from things that might harm it.

Alcohol is not good for the brain.
When people drink too much alcohol
their brains stop working well.
They lose their sense of balance,
their coordination,
and their memory.
They may get angry
for no reason,
or just act silly.

Some drugs are very bad for your brain.
Remember that brain cells
send messages to each other
by chemistry.
If dangerous chemicals reach the brain
the messages will get mixed up.

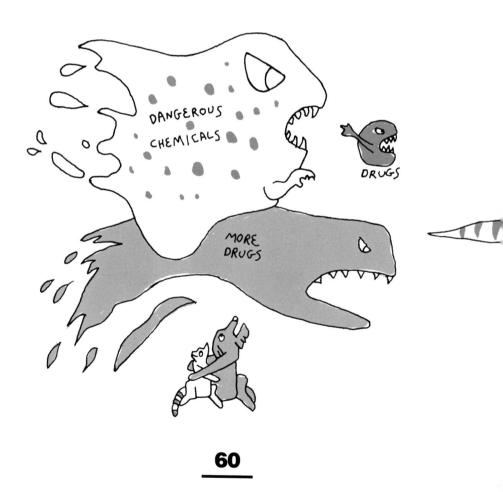

That is why some illegal drugs
such as LSD, cocaine, and marijuana
make you see things
that aren't really there,
or make you frightened or angry
for no reason.
Even if the drugs make you happy,
they may be damaging your brain cells—
and remember,
you can't get new ones!

There is no computer that can do
all the things your brain can do.
Take good care of it and use it, too!

GLOSSARY

BRAIN STEM: The part of the brain that makes the body work automatically. It also connects the cerebrum and cerebellum with the spinal cord.

BRAIN WAVES: Patterns formed by recordings of the electricity in the neurons close to the surface of the cerebrum.

CEREBELLUM: The part of the brain that controls coordination and balance.

CEREBRUM: The biggest part of the human brain. It is the part where thoughts are formed.

GLIAL CELLS: Cells in the brain that hold the neurons in place and help to nourish them.

NEURON: A nerve cell consisting of a body, a long tail, and many branches. A neuron can send messages to other neurons or to other cells in the body.

SPINAL CORD: A cord made up of nerve cells that connect the brain with most other parts of the body.

BERTEL BRUUN was born in Skelskør, Denmark and studied at the University of Copenhagen, where he received an M.D. He was trained in neurology at the Neurological Institute of New York and is now an assistant clinical professor of neurology at Columbia University. Dr. Bruun is the author of many medical articles and of twelve books on birds (a life-long avocation), including *Animals: The Strange and Exciting Story of Their Lives.* He is also co-author of *The Human Body* with his wife, Ruth.

RUTH BRUUN grew up in New York City and received an M.D. from Cornell University, where she is now a clinical associate professor of psychiatry. She has co-authored two books and written many articles on medical subjects. Dr. Bruun is also co-author of *The Human Body,* which won a National Science Teacher's Association/Children's Book Council Joint Committee award for outstanding science book in 1982. The Bruuns have six children, one of whom is the artist, Peter.

PETER BRUUN was graduated from Williams College and has an M.F.A. in painting from the Maryland Institute College of Art. He has been a freelance illustrator for newspapers and magazines. Mr. Bruun lives in Baltimore with his wife Serafina. This is his first children's book.